DATE DUE

IMMIGRATION

How Should It Be Controlled?

Meish Goldish

Twenty-First Century Books

A Division of Henry Holt and Company
New York

Twenty-First Century Books
A division of Henry Holt and Company, Inc.
115 West 18th Street
New York, New York 10011

Henry Holt® and colophon are trademarks of Henry Holt and Company, Inc.
Publishers since 1866

Published in Canada by Fitzhenry & Whiteside Ltd.
195 Allstate Parkway, Markham, Ontario L3R 4T8

Printed in the United States of America
All first editions are printed on acid-free paper ∞.

Created and produced in association with Blackbirch Graphics, Inc.

Library of Congress Cataloging-in-Publication Data

Goldish, Meish.
    Immigration: how should it be controlled / Meish Goldish. — 1st ed.
        p.   cm. — (Issues of our time)
    Includes bibliographical references and index.
    ISBN 0-8050-3182-0 (alk. paper)
    1. United States—Emigration and immigration—Government policy—Juvenile
literature. 2. United States—Emigration and immigration—Juvenile literature.
[1. United States—Emigration and immigration.] I. Title. II. Series.
JV6493.G65   1994
325.73—dc20   93-43513
                                                                    CIP
                                                                    AC

Contents

. . . . .

Who Should Be Let In?

"Give me your tired, your poor,
Your huddled masses yearning to breathe free,
The wretched refuse of your teeming shore.
Send these, the homeless, tempest-tost to me,
I lift my lamp beside the golden door!"

These words, from the poem "The New Colossus" by Emma Lazarus, appear at the base of the Statue of Liberty in New York Harbor. Since 1886, the statue has greeted millions of immigrants who have sailed to America to begin new lives. The poem reflects America's tradition of welcoming newcomers. Even before Lady Liberty arrived, immigrants were pouring onto U.S. shores. As a result, the United States is known as "a nation of immigrants."

Every person now living in the United States can trace his or her heritage to another country. Even Native Americans, here long before the first Europeans, were immigrants. Historians believe that Native Americans came across a land bridge between Siberia and Alaska during the Ice Age.

It may seem surprising, then, that some Americans feel immigration should either be ended, or sharply curbed. Yet that is the case. Many citizens believe that too many immigrants are entering the country. Concerned with an ailing economy and overcrowded cities, anti-immigration groups want to reduce the number of people that are taken in.

Others disagree with this idea. They argue that America has always been a nation of immigrants. They believe it would be selfish to suddenly close the door on people. Many who favor immigration believe that barring aliens of any nationality is shameful racism.

Historians know that the debate over immigration is nothing new. Questions of immigration refer to events as far back as the *Mayflower* landing at Plymouth Rock in 1620: "Who should be let in?" and "How many people is too many?" Today's debate has become much more heated. The numbers of immigrants coming to the United States are now reaching record levels. This book will help you to understand all the issues involved.

For over a century, the Statue of Liberty has been a symbol of freedom for immigrants who come to America.

1

......

People on the Move

It was early in the morning on June 6, 1993. The waters off the Rockaway Peninsula, in New York City, were rolling wildly. In the turbulent ocean, a large cargo steamer called the *Golden Venture* approached land, trying to reach the shore in the darkness. Suddenly, about 200 yards from shore, the rusty, 150-foot-long vessel struck a sandbar. Cargo began spilling everywhere. But in this case, the cargo was not oil or other consumable goods. It was a group of people—about 280 Chinese passengers who were being smuggled into the United States.

When the boat crashed, the people on board panicked. They leaped into the stormy waters,

The *Golden Venture* traveled 17,000 miles before running aground near New York City. Many immigrants will risk their lives for a chance to have a brighter future.

screaming and struggling for their lives. At least ten people died in their efforts to reach land. The others were rescued by New York City police, the Coast Guard, and U.S. immigration agents. Not surprisingly, the Chinese were terrified—not only by their traumatic landing, but by the fear they would be returned home. "I would rather live in an American jail than go back to the rice fields of China," one man said.

As passengers were questioned over the next several days, horror stories emerged about their voyage. They had traveled 17,000 miles from Bangkok, Thailand, starting out nearly half a year earlier. During the long trip they received only one meal a day, often just a plate of rotten rice. There were no showers and only one toilet. People slept

Officials aid in the rescue efforts for the Chinese immigrants from the *Golden Venture*. Many of these illegal aliens used their life savings to pay for this treacherous passage to the United States.

on cots or on the bare deck. Yet for the "privilege" of sailing on the *Golden Venture,* each passenger paid about $30,000. Despite their suffering, most were happy. Why? These Chinese came to the United States for the same reason that most immigrants have come to America over the past 400 years—to escape poverty, suffering, and oppression in their own country, and to make better lives for themselves. For centuries, America has been known universally as the "land of opportunity."

Of course, most immigrants do not normally travel as hidden cargo. They travel by plane, by car, on foot, or by ship, and register with the proper authorities before and after their arrival. Other immigrants come to the United States under emergency circumstances. And some are brought against their will. In order to fully understand the current debate about immigration, it is important to know the meaning of the term.

Different Kinds
of Immigrants
Immigration is defined as "the act of coming to a new country or region in order to settle there." If you and your family go abroad on vacation, you are not immigrating, because you are staying for only a short period. Immigration means moving permanently, or at least for a substantial amount of time.

Immigration is the movement *to* a new country. Leaving one's original country is called emigration. In the case of the *Golden Venture* passengers, they were emigrating *from* China and immigrating *to* America.

Immigrants can be divided into four main categories. Most people who arrive in this country are legal immigrants. That means they follow all the proper procedures for moving from their native country to America. Potential immigrants to the United States go to the American consulate in their homeland to apply for a permanent visa, or passport. Upon arriving in America, they apply for permanent residence, which allows them to work legally. After five years, they can apply for citizenship.

A second category of immigrants are refugees. These are people who leave their homeland due to political or religious persecution, war, or disasters such as famine and disease. They seek asylum, or protection, in the country to which they flee. In the past, the United States has accepted millions of refugees, such as those who fled the Communist takeover of Cuba in 1959 or the Vietnam War in the 1970s. Refugees in America can be traced back to the Pilgrims, who sought religious freedom from the Church of England in 1620.

A third category of immigrants are forced immigrants. These are individuals who are brought to

another country against their will. Until about 1800, America practiced forced immigration by accepting millions of black Africans, who were shipped here to become slaves. Although slavery was outlawed in 1865, an illegal form of immigrant slavery now exists in the United States. You will read more about this issue later in the book.

A fourth category of immigrants are illegal aliens. These are people who enter a new country without following the procedures required by law. The passengers on the *Golden Venture* are one example of illegal aliens. Officials estimate that of the 1 million immigrants who come to the United States annually, more than 200,000 enter illegally. You will learn more about the issue of illegal immigration in Chapter Three.

The Pilgrims were the first refugees to come to America. They wanted to live in a country where they could practice their religion freely.

The Waves of Immigration

Despite the different opinions people hold about immigration, one fact is clear: America has always been a home for immigrants. The history of American immigration can be tracked in four main arrival periods, or "waves."

The first wave began in the early 1600s, when English colonists, along with some indentured servants, settled along the eastern shore of what is now the United States. Other colonists came from France, Germany, Ireland, Italy, Poland, Scotland, and Sweden. Many were refugees seeking to escape religious and political persecution. Between 1700 and the start of the Revolutionary War in 1775, some 450,000 immigrants arrived on American shores. In addition, 375,000 black slaves were brought involuntarily to work on large cotton and tobacco plantations in the South.

The second wave of immigration lasted from around 1820 to 1875. During that period, nearly 8 million immigrants arrived in America.

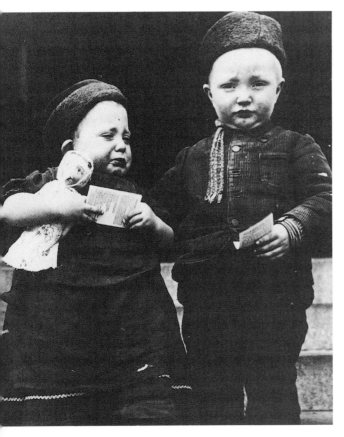

During the late 1800s and early 1900s, millions of immigrants, such as these Dutch children and their family, came to America from Europe.

They hailed mainly from northern and western Europe. About a third were Irish and another third were German. The Irish came to escape a potato famine that occurred in Ireland in the 1840s. And the Germans suffered from both unemployment and political tyranny in their homeland. During this wave, more than 150,000 Chinese also immigrated to America. Many were eager to get rich in the California gold rush of the 1850s.

The third wave lasted from 1881 to 1920. More than 24 million immigrants moved to America during this time. At first they came from northern

The Long Journey from Afghanistan to America

In 1979, when Abdul was seven years old, his father decided the family must leave their home in Afghanistan. The year before, a military group financed by the Soviet Union had taken over the government. Many Afghans opposed the new rule, believing its policies conflicted with their religious beliefs. Fighting broke out, making the country unsafe for civilians.

When rumors of a Soviet invasion spread, Abdul's family made their move. In the middle of the night, smugglers drove them across the border into Iran in a truck. Two months later, the Soviet army entered Afghanistan. The family was convinced they had been wise to leave. But their troubles were far from over. Being in Iran illegally, Abdul was thrown out of school after two weeks. He was forced to work as a plumber's assistant.

The family remained in Iran for six years. Then the father decided they would move to the United States. Having no legal papers, they traveled to Pakistan and applied for visas at the American Embassy. They had to live at the embassy with other families for several months while waiting for their visas. During that time, Abdul's father died. Finally, in 1986, Abdul arrived safely in America with his mother, brothers, and sisters.

In 1989, Soviet troops withdrew from Afghanistan. But by then, the war there had created more than three million Afghan refugees—like Abdul—who had fled to a variety of other countries.

and western Europe, but later more came from southern and eastern Europe. Worsening conditions in their homelands caused most of these immigrants to seek a better life in a new country. Most Jews wanted to get away from religious persecution. Many Poles came to escape poverty and an outbreak of an intestinal disease called cholera. Italians, Austrians, Czechs, and Hungarians, for the most part, all wished to avoid poverty and overpopulation in their countries. Many Danes, Norwegians, and Swedes left their homes because of a shortage of farmland.

The fourth wave of immigration began in 1965 and continues to the present. So far, over 20 million immigrants have arrived during this period. Many experts predict the fourth wave will ultimately have the greatest effect on the overall makeup of America. The current wave includes 2 million Mexicans, who have come to the United States to escape both poverty and unemployment in their country. One million Dominicans, Haitians, and Jamaicans have immigrated for the same reasons. And nearly a million Cubans and over half a million Vietnamese have fled political persecution in their homelands. Today, more than a million immigrants continue to pour into the United States annually.

Currently, a debate rages over the large numbers of immigrants who are being admitted to America.

Can the country accommodate so many new arrivals? Does the United States have an obligation to grant them entry? Or is it time to say, "Sorry, no vacancy"? These are not easy questions. But clues to a few of the answers may be found by looking at America's immigration laws, both past and present.

The Flood from China

In recent years, there has been a sharp increase in the number of Chinese immigrants coming to America. Why? Largely it is due to political developments in China. In 1989, students, workers, and other Chinese citizens held mass demonstrations in Beijing's Tiananmen Square. They rallied for democracy and called for an end to government corruption. The Chinese army crushed the demonstrations and killed hundreds of protesters. Later, large numbers of suspected antigovernment sympathizers were arrested, and many were put to death.

After the Tiananmen Square massacre, U.S. president Bush sought to make emigration from China easier. Congress passed new laws that would allow refugees from China to come to America quickly and escape political persecution.

A second important development has also affected Chinese immigration. The Chinese government, concerned with overpopulation, has established a new birth policy. In general, it forbids Chinese couples from having more than one child. In some cases, sterilization or abortion are ordered by the government to enforce the ruling. Upset by the decree, the

Beijing residents look on as the Chinese army stands ready to stop demonstrations for democracy in Tiananmen Square.

Bush administration declared that Chinese refugees persecuted by the new policy could come to America.

As a result of Tiananmen Square and the Chinese birth policy, thousands of Chinese aliens have sought political asylum in the United States in recent years. Since 1989, about 85 percent of their requests have been granted. In 1992—out of 3,440 applications for asylum—only 89 were denied.

2

Immigration: What's the Law?

The United States has seen many changes in its immigration laws. In the Colonial Era of the 1600s and 1700s, there were no regulations at all. The country was large, and there was plenty of room for new arrivals. Europeans were warmly welcomed in the East, as were the Spanish who settled in the Southwest.

But in the mid-1800s, some Americans began to object to America's "open door" immigration policy. Settlers were now spread from coast to coast. Job opportunities and available land seemed to be declining. A movement known as nativism began to grow. Nativists wanted to restrict immigration to America. They formed political groups like the Know-Nothing Party,

Legal immigrants attend a swearing-in ceremony that will officially make them U.S. citizens. This is the final step in a long process that is required to attain citizenship in America.

which grew in power in the 1850s. The nativists protested the continued immigration of the Germans and the Irish. In time, resentment also grew against the Chinese, who had helped build the railroads and work the mines during the 1860s and 1870s. Many people accused the Chinese of taking jobs away from American laborers. Eventually, anti-Chinese sentiment led to violence. In one Los Angeles riot in 1871, 21 Chinese were lynched or shot, and in a riot in San Francisco's Chinatown in 1877, 25 Chinese businesses were burned.

Bans and Quotas

As a result of growing nativism, the United States passed its first national immigration laws in 1875. They banned convicts and prostitutes from entering the country. Later the ban was extended to include "lunatics," "idiots," and arrivals who seemed unable to support themselves. Soon after, restrictions were declared based on nationality. In 1882, Congress passed the Chinese Exclusion Act. It forbade Chinese laborers from entering the United States, and denied citizenship to Chinese aliens who were already living in the country. In 1907, a similar ban—called the Gentlemen's Agreement—also kept out Japanese laborers.

In 1921, the United States placed its first quotas, or number limits, on immigrants. The quotas said that for each year, new arrivals from any country could not exceed three percent of the people from that country who lived in the United States. This meant that if 4 million first-generation Germans were already in the

This 1921 political cartoon illustrates the artist's perception of the first U.S. quotas on immigration. The law was passed to limit the number of immigrants coming to the United States from Europe.

United States, then no more than 120,000 Germans a year could enter. In 1924, stricter quotas were established. Congress said it wished to maintain the "racial preponderance of the basic strain of our people." In other words, it wanted America to remain a white Anglo-Saxon nation.

But not everyone was pleased with the quotas. Many Americans disliked the idea. They felt it was political racism. After many years, the laws were changed. Because China was an ally during World War II, the United States dropped its ban on Chinese immigration after the war. The Refugee Relief Act of 1953 enabled about 600,000 European and Russian citizens, left homeless by World War II, to enter the United States.

In 1965, an important new immigration law was passed in the United States. It ended quotas based on nationality. Now immigrants were counted according to the region they came from. The number of immigrants from Europe and Central America was already high, so fewer people from those regions were allowed in. In contrast, the number of immigrants from Asia, Haiti, and Cuba was low, so huge numbers of these refugees began arriving on U.S. shores in the 1970s. A Refugee Act was then passed in 1980 that raised the quota for these refugees to 50,000 that year. It was later extended to cover the 142,000 refugees who arrived in the 1990s.

In 1990, new laws further increased the total number of immigrants allowed into the United States. A ceiling of 700,000 per year was set for 1992 to 1994. The law put no limit, however, on the number of relatives of U.S. citizens who could enter the country. It also did not include refugees.

Today, Americans debate the current quotas. Anti-immigration groups say that America has neither the space nor the money to support so many immigrants. Pro-immigration groups feel quotas should be eliminated, to bring more foreign talent and cultural diversity to America. They maintain that ending quotas would stop illegal immigration.

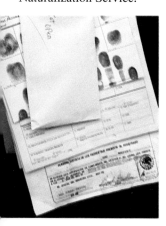

A legal immigrant submits an application for permanent residency that will be reviewed for accuracy by the Immigration and Naturalization Service.

Laws of Citizenship

Immigrants who seek to become U.S. citizens go through a lengthy process. They first must enter the United States legally, by applying for admission through the American consulate in their home country. People wishing to join relatives who are U.S. citizens—or who possess work skills needed in the United States—may have short waits. But others might wait years for admission into the United States, especially in countries where many people have already submitted immigration applications.

Once in the United States, an alien applies

This U.S. immigration office in Houston, Texas—like others around the country— receives thousands of applications for permanent residence each year. Immigrants who pass this stage of the process will be granted green cards.

for permanent residence. The application is then reviewed by the Immigration and Naturalization Service (INS). The INS is a government agency that enforces the immigration laws and policies set by Congress. If the INS verifies all the necessary information, permanent residence is granted. The immigrant then receives an alien registration card, often referred to as a "green card." (The card used to be green but the color has since changed.) A green card entitles registered aliens to work legally

The Ordeal of the "Boat People"

Haitians detained at Guantanamo Naval Base in Cuba.

The country of Haiti has suffered much political unrest in the past. Since the 1970s, tens of thousands of Haitians have left the country due to political turmoil and a failing economy. Many have sought refuge in the United States.

But in the 1990s, a new complication arose. In September 1991, Haiti's president, the Reverend Jean-Bertrand Aristide, was overthrown. Soldiers began shooting at people. Many were killed because of their political beliefs. Fearing for their lives, more than 40,000 Haitians sailed in rickety boats to the United States. President Bush ordered the "boat people" detained at Guantanamo Naval Base in Cuba, where their claims for asylum could be processed. More than 10,000 of the arrivals were declared political refugees, and were allowed to enter the United States. The rest were deemed economic refugees (people leaving to escape poverty) and were sent back to Haiti.

But of the 10,000 that were allowed into America, about 200 were found to have HIV, the virus that causes AIDS. This set off a great debate among Americans. Should the HIV-positive refugees be allowed into the United States, along with the others? Some Americans said no, feeling these Haitians were health risks. Others said yes, because their lawful rights were otherwise being denied. For 20 months, the Haitians were held at the naval base in Cuba before a U.S. judge ordered them brought to the United States. The Haitians knew that not all Americans welcomed them, but most were pleased just to be in America. As one refugee said, "At least I am alive. If I was in Haiti, I would have been killed."

in the United States and extends to them most of the rights of the U.S. Constitution. Green card holders are required to pay taxes, and males must register for the selective service if a draft is in effect. Immigrants who are denied permanent residence can appeal their case in court. But if they lose, they must then leave the country.

After living in the United States for five years (or three years if the immigrant is married to a U.S. citizen) a permanent resident may then apply for citizenship. This process is called naturalization. The applicant fills out a form that asks questions about residence, past employment, marital status, military service, and criminal records. Then the applicant usually waits several months for an interview date. The interview includes a written test on both American history and government. Typical questions might be: "Who was the president during the Civil War?" or "How many senators are there in the U.S. Senate?" Applicants who pass this test report for a swearing-in ceremony for citizenship, usually a month or two after the interview.

Participants place their green card applications in bins outside a Virginia post office during a 1991 lottery that awarded 40,000 winners permanent residence.

Under U.S. law, permanent residents are not required to become citizens. But without citizenship, certain privileges are lost. For example, noncitizens cannot vote, serve on juries, hold public office, travel for unlimited time abroad, or sponsor parents or siblings who wish to enter the United States.

Policies in Other Countries
Immigration laws differ from country to country. New laws often reflect the changing attitudes of a nation's government and people. For example, before the 1960s, Australia favored British and North American immigrants, practicing a "white Australian" policy. But today that policy has been relaxed. Australia now accepts many immigrants from India and other Asian countries. In Israel, any Jewish immigrant is granted citizenship under its "law of return."

A popular destination for immigrants is Canada. Until the 1960s, Canadian immigration laws favored people of British descent. Today, however, arrivals are admitted regardless of national origin, religion, race, or sex. Priority is given to refugees and to relatives of Canadian citizens. Others are judged by a point system that estimates their ability to adapt to Canadian life. Points are given for factors such as the immigrant's age, education, job skills, and language ability.

"The Isle of Hope and Tears"

When immigrants arrived in this country a century ago, they did not simply walk off the boat and into the streets. They first had to be "processed," or officially registered. Processing—which began in 1855—helped to ensure that people with dangerous diseases or suspicious backgrounds were not granted entry to America. For most arrivals from Europe, processing took place at Ellis Island, near the Statue of Liberty in New York Harbor. From 1892 to 1924, some 12 million immigrants passed through Ellis Island—about 5,000 a day. For most, it was a frightening experience. The new arrivals generally spoke little English, and did not know what to expect in an unknown land. Doctors first examined them for illness. Many had become sick as a result of the long, difficult voyage they had just taken. Sick immigrants were checked for contagious diseases such as leprosy and tuberculosis. Those with suspicious symptoms had "T.D." marked on their coats in chalk. It stood for "temporarily detained." If they failed a second exam, they were put on ships and sent back to their native country.

After the physical examination, immigration officials asked them questions: "How much money do you have?" or "How do you plan to earn a living in America?" Newcomers had to prove they could support themselves, even though most had come to America because of poverty in their homeland. They were also questioned about their political beliefs. Suspected criminals had "S.I." marked on their clothes. It stood for "special inquiry." They were held for further questioning, and were often deported, or sent home. Those who seemed unable to support themselves were marked "L.P.C.," or "likely public charge." These immigrants were also deported. Because of the fear that filled new immigrants, Ellis Island was nicknamed "The Isle of Hope and Tears."

In 1954, Ellis Island was closed. After renovation and repair, the site re-opened as a public museum in 1990. Visitors can see photographs, clothing, and passports that belonged to the immigrants. A Wall of Honor lists the names of some 200,000 immigrants who passed through Ellis Island.

The Wall of Honor at Ellis Island.

3
·······

Illegal Aliens

The Immigration and Naturalization Service says the most serious problem it faces today is illegal aliens. INS officials estimate that from 200,000 to 500,000 people enter the United States illegally each year. There may be anywhere from 3 to 12 million illegals now living in the country. Generally, they come for the same reasons that other immigrants come—to find better jobs and to improve their lives. But unlike legal immigrants, they do not follow the set procedures for entry. Thus they avoid years of waiting and possible rejection of their applications. In order to appreciate the serious concerns about illegal aliens, you must first understand how they get into the country.

Illegal aliens are detained by the INS in San Francisco after their ship was captured near the Golden Gate Bridge. Many immigrants try to enter the United States undetected.

Unlawful

Entry   People seeking to enter the United States illegally use a variety of methods. Perhaps the best known approach is sneaking across the border. The United States has about 8,000 miles of borders. But the Border Patrol, a division of the INS, does not have enough agents to always monitor the territory effectively. Most of the problem occurs along the U.S.-Mexico border. Every year, for example, more than 100,000 Mexicans manage to pass undetected into California, Arizona, New Mexico, and Texas. The U.S.-Mexico border is about 2,000 miles long. But the border patrol has fewer than 4,000 agents to cover the area—less than two agents per mile. Even

A border patrol agent monitors the traffic at the U. S.-Mexico border. Annually, thousands of illegal Mexican immigrants manage to enter the United States by using phony I.D.s and other documents.

though guards use sophisticated night-sight equipment, many illegal aliens still manage to escape detection. Similarly, immigrants from overseas often hide in ships that are traveling to the United States, hoping to land in America without being detected by Coast Guard patrols.

Illegal entry is also gained by presenting immigration officials with counterfeit visas, passports, and other documents. U.S. passports are frequently stolen and are then altered with a photograph of the illegal alien. In Haiti, fake U.S. visas are often sold openly on the street. Phony I.D.s such as Social Security cards and driver's licenses are easily available in the United States and sell for as little as $500. Sometimes I.D. cards are not even required. As one illegal alien confessed, "When an employer or whoever asks for your social security number, you just make it up."

A newer method of illegal entry today is asking for political asylum when the claim is not legitimate. When Chinese are smuggled into America, for example, they are trained to say—if caught— that they seek asylum because of China's restrictive birth policies. Illegal aliens may use that excuse, even if they are not planning to marry or to have any children. Other Chinese claim to be refugees of the Tiananmen Square uprising of 1989, even though they are not. Under American law, each request for political asylum must be carefully re-viewed. Illegal aliens know that processing their appeals can take several years, giving them time to establish their lives in America. The jails are full, so asylum seekers are frequently released, and many simply vanish into society. About 30 percent never show up for their court dates.

A Dangerous Situation

Immigrants who slip past authorities often are unaware of the problems and dangers that lie ahead of them. Many Mexicans, for example, take jobs as migrant farm workers in California. Employers who hire them do so because they can pay them less than American laborers. And since the immigrants are illegal, employers can also avoid paying them health benefits. Often the working conditions are unsafe, but there is little the illegals can do to protect themselves. They are afraid to complain to authorities because they themselves are lawbreakers. Employers frequently take advantage of them. One illegal worked 36 hours straight, then was docked a day's pay for taking a one-hour nap.

Today, Chinese illegals face even greater danger in the United States. Many are brought in by Asian smugglers called "snakeheads." The immigrants agree to pay from $30,000 to $50,000 for passage to

A Mexican finds work picking cherries on a farm. Illegal immigrants who work as migrant farm laborers are most often underpaid, work in unsafe conditions, and are not given health insurance. Since they are not American citizens, they are not protected by U.S. laws.

America. But after arriving, they find America is not the "golden land" they imagined. They are often forced to work in restaurants and laundries for as little as two dollars an hour. After working 16 or 18 hours a day, 7 days a week, many still cannot make enough to pay off the snakeheads. When that happens, the illegals are kidnapped and high ransoms are demanded from their relatives. While being held, often for months or even years, captives are tortured. If the kidnappers do not receive the ransom money, the aliens are sometimes killed. Some victims are forced to sell drugs, and others are forced into prostitution. "This is a modern-day slave trade," said one advocate for immigrants.

Looking for Solutions

What can be done about the problems of illegal immigration? In recent years, the U.S. government has searched for ways to stop the flow of illegals. In 1986, Congress passed the Immigration Reform and Control Act. It imposes large fines and prison terms on employers who hire illegal aliens. It also requires employers to ask job seekers for proof that they are U.S. citizens or aliens eligible for work in the United States. At first the new law seemed to be effective. Arrests by the U.S. Border Patrol dropped from 1.7 million in 1985 to half of that in 1988. Because employers were very

The Nanny Problem

Illegal aliens may face arrest and deportation if they are caught. But people who employ illegals also run risks. Two people who learned this lesson were Zoe Baird and Kimba Wood. After Bill Clinton took office as president of the United States in 1993, he nominated Zoe Baird, a lawyer, to serve as attorney general. But during her confirmation hearings, it was discovered that Baird had hired an illegal alien as a nanny, or babysitter. As a result, her nomination was withdrawn. When Clinton next nominated Judge Kimba Wood for attorney general, she had a similar problem. Wood had technically done nothing wrong, since she hired her babysitter before 1986, when the law was passed against hiring illegals. But even the appearance of wrongdoing made Clinton change his mind.

These two highly publicized cases called attention to the difficulty of following the law exactly. Employers can only hire people who are legally eligible for work. In order for aliens to be eligible, they need to have a green card. But the card may not arrive for six or seven years after the application has been filed. Until then, the alien is technically not allowed to work. In Zoe Baird's case, she had applied for a green card for her nanny, but it had not yet come through. But if all parents waited the necessary years until the green card came, they might not need a nanny at all. "Almost everybody in the United States is violating the law," said one immigration lawyer. Many believe the solution is for Congress to pass a new law enabling aliens to work on a temporary basis, even without a green card.

Many see the present law as a hardship on working mothers since they must find someone to care for their children during the day. As one immigration lawyer put it, "The law would be different if Congress were fifty percent female."

Zoe Baird speaks after being nominated for attorney general. She lost her nomination when it was discovered that the woman she employed as a nanny did not have a green card.

reluctant to hire illegals, fewer tried to cross into the United States. But by 1992, the number of arrests had risen to 1.2 million. As a rule, for every illegal who is caught, two or three manage to sneak through. About 3 million aliens a year get across the border. Today, many Americans say that the 1986 law is not effective. They are calling for stricter penalties for both illegals and their employers.

Guarding the seas has also proven difficult. Since 1991, U.S. officials have spotted over 40 ships carrying Asian aliens to America. More than half were stopped, but others continue to come. One INS agent said, "We can't send our people, like Barbary pirates, out to intercept vessels on the high seas. There are too many oceans, too many ships." Some countries have accused the United States of breaking the law by intercepting ships in waters outside its jurisdiction. But a Supreme Court ruling in 1993 upheld the government's action.

Many Americans feel that more severe penalties are needed for those convicted of alien smuggling. The *Golden Venture* operators can receive a maximum of 5 years in prison if they are convicted. Some people would like to see the penalty stiffened to 20 years in prison. They are also calling for more frequent confiscation (the act of property being seized by authorities) of ships that are involved in smuggling illegal aliens. The *Golden Venture* was confiscated during the investigation of that case. The United States is seeking the cooperation of other nations in fighting illegals on the ocean. In 1993, when three ships with more than 650 Chinese aliens were found approaching California, the United States ordered them to Mexico. The Mexican government, which has stricter immigration laws than America, then deported the Chinese. Had the ships landed on U.S. shores, hearings would have been required by law for all passengers seeking political asylum.

Despite these events, some immigrants' rights groups maintain that illegal immigration is not a problem. They say that illegals, like legals, simply seek a better life, and should not be treated as outlaws. They point out that illegal immigration could be stopped by declaring all immigration legal. In

Illegal Chinese immigrants are held in San Pedro, California. Although authorities try to intercept ships carrying illegal aliens before they enter U.S. territory, many vessels still manage to get through.

By proposing a larger budget for the INS, President Clinton hopes to decrease the number of illegal aliens who arrive in the United States.

one respect, the 1986 law satisfied them. This law gave amnesty, or pardon, to all illegals who could prove they had been living in America since before 1982. As a result, some 3.5 million illegals became legal by 1988, when the period of amnesty ended. But those opposed to the idea of amnesty say it encourages further illegal immigration.

Currently, the U.S. government is determined to bring its borders under control. In 1993, President Clinton proposed increasing the INS budget by $172 million to beef up the U.S. Border Patrol, and to crack down on fraud by issuing specially processed (harder to counterfeit) visa photos. The government is also seeking faster processing of asylum claims, to prevent phony applicants from remaining in the country and then disappearing.

Other countries are seeking similar solutions. Canada, like the United States, has been flooded with phony refugee requests in recent years. As in the United States, each case must be heard. In 1988, the Canadian government passed a new law intended to reduce the time required for hearings and decisions. But by 1991, over 75,000 claims waited to be processed. Many Canadians feel the new law has not proven to be effective. As a result, a significant number are calling for an amnesty that would allow all backlogged refugees to live in Canada as citizens.

A Sheik Sparks New Anger Against Aliens

Sheik Omar Abdel Rahman.

In February 1993, a powerful bomb exploded in a parking lot beneath the World Trade Center, a set of 110-story twin business towers in New York City. Six people died in the blast, and thousands of workers had to be evacuated from the building through heavy smoke. An extensive police investigation led to the arrests of several Egyptian Muslims, who were charged with planning and carrying out the bombing. All the accused were found to be followers of Sheik Omar Abdel Rahman, a blind, 55-year-old Egyptian cleric based in Jersey City, New Jersey. In August 1993, Abdel Rahman was arrested for conspiring in the attack after being held by authorities who discovered he was an illegal alien.

The sheik's case highlighted how easily illegal aliens can come and go in the United States. According to government officials, Abdel Rahman entered the United States from the Sudan in 1990 with a visa that should not have been issued, as he was on a government watch list for his involvement with Islamic radicals. When the sheik applied for a green card in 1991, immigration agents were fooled because he used the last name "Ali" on the application.

In 1992, officials revoked Abdel Rahman's permanent resident-alien status, saying he had lied on his application about past arrests and about having more than one wife. Both are grounds for deportation. But by then, authorities had unknowingly let the sheik enter and leave the country four times.

In August 1993, the sheik was being held in a Federal prison in New York State, as U.S. immigration officials worked to have him deported to Egypt. At the same time, plans were also being made to put the sheik and some of his followers on trial for the World Trade Center bombing.

4
······

Is Immigration Good for America?

In a 1993 *Newsweek* magazine poll, 60 percent of the people questioned said that they felt immigration was bad for America now. Interestingly, the same people said that they thought immigration had been good for the country in the past. What caused their change in attitude?

There are several factors. One reason is the economy. Generally, whenever unemployment is high, so are anti-immigration feelings. Some people believe that foreigners take jobs away from native-born laborers. They also accuse immigrants of being a burden on the taxpayer. A second, more recent, factor is terrorism. Arthur Helton, an immigration expert from the Lawyers Committee for Human Rights, said in

Albert Einstein, an immigrant from Germany, is a compelling example of the positive effect that immigration has had on the United States.

a *New York Times* interview, "If you can picture the image of the Statue of Liberty dissolving, and being replaced by the image of the World Trade Center after it was bombed, you have the sense of the negative trends in the current debate."

With more Americans calling for less immigration, the question of the benefits of immigration deserves careful study.

Building the Nation

Pro-immigration groups say it is impossible to ignore the benefits of immigration. America, they maintain, grew by the muscle and sweat of its immigrants. They built the nation's railroads, toiled in its sweatshops, and dug its mines. Today, many industries such as hotels, garment factories, and restaurants, continue to thrive on foreign labor.

But anti-immigrationists disagree. They claim that the benefits of foreign labor no longer exist. Years ago, more jobs were available, so immigrants were welcome. But today, with increased automation and technology, there are fewer jobs to be had. In California, where thousands of Mexicans and Asians flood the job market, unemployment rose to almost 10 percent in 1993. This forced many native Californians to leave the state to search for work elsewhere. Why are aliens getting the jobs?

Immigrant laborers, such as these coal miners working in Virginia in 1908, have made a great contribution to the building of our country.

Because they are willing to work for lower wages than American laborers. This drives down the labor market, eventually forcing everyone to settle for lower wages.

Pro-immigration groups take a different view. They argue that immigrants get their jobs because Americans are not willing to take them. The work is perceived as demeaning or unattractive. If aliens were not allowed to fill the positions, no one would.

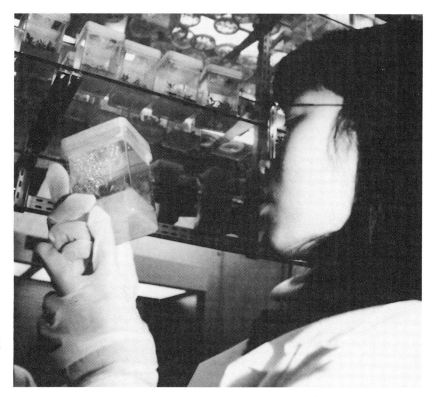

Today, many immigrants who come to America have advanced degrees and valuable technological skills. Their knowledge helps America continue to grow as a nation.

Farm owners say that without foreign labor, their crops would rot in their fields. In addition, many people feel a low-wage labor system is positive, since it makes America more competitive in the world market.

Besides, pro-immigrationists add, not all aliens work at low-paying, unskilled jobs. Many come to America with a special talent that is badly needed by the nation. In 1991, some 23,000 immigrants were admitted to the United States based on their job skills. Experts say that number could rise to 85,000 by 1995. America needs more scientists, engineers, and medical technicians. Immigrants can help provide that talent. Imagine if German-born scientist Albert Einstein or Scottish-born inventor Alexander Graham Bell had been denied entry to the country. Think of the benefits America would have lost.

The Immigrant Who Wrote "God Bless America"

Many Americans consider "God Bless America" to be one of the most patriotic songs ever written. But what they may not know is that the song, along with dozens of other popular American tunes, was penned by a foreign-born composer.

His name was Israel Baline, born in Russia in 1888. In the early 1890s, Israel and his family left their home to escape religious persecution. The Balines came to America during the third wave of immigration—from 1881 to about 1920. Israel found a new home in New York City. Like many other new arrivals of the era, he also received a new name. Israel Baline was "Americanized" to Irving Berlin.

Very quickly, Berlin proved himself a composer with special talent. His first hit was "Alexander's Ragtime Band" in 1911. The song introduced a new sound that combined American folk music with a rhythmic style called ragtime. Berlin went on to enjoy a brilliant career, writing popular songs, tunes for Broadway shows, and melodies for Hollywood movies. Among his best known hits are "White Christmas," "Easter Parade," and "There's No Business Like Show Business."

Irving Berlin demonstrated an extraordinary appreciation for America during his life. After "God Bless America" became a huge success, Berlin wished to show his gratitude to the country that had enabled him to thrive artistically. He donated all royalties from the song to the Boy Scouts of America.

Irving Berlin.

Understanding
Each Other   The benefits of immigration do
not stop at labor. There is also the matter of cultural
understanding. Those who favor immigration say
that those who oppose it suffer from xenophobia,
a fear of foreigners. It is a fear that is caused by
unfamiliarity with the ways of strangers. Pro-
immigrationists say that the world will never
improve if different groups do not develop a better
understanding and appreciation of one another by
living together, side by side.

But others disagree. They say that most ethnic
groups do not live side by side, so a cultural ex-
change is impossible. America, they maintain, is no
longer a "melting pot," where people of various
backgrounds once came together and adopted a
single way of life. Today, new arrivals cling to their
roots and resist becoming "Americanized." Instead
of being a "melting pot," the nation is more like a
"salad bowl," where each foreign group retains its
own distinctive characteristics.

History tends to back up this claim. A century
ago, most immigrants to America were white Europeans. Their race and culture were similar to those
of Americans, who mainly came from Europe them-

Opposite:
The varied cultures that
make up the United States
are embodied in this
everyday crowd scene
in New York City.

selves. The immigrants' goal was to assimilate, or
mix, with American society. Today, however, most
immigrants are not white Europeans. They are

largely Mexicans, Filipinos, Koreans, Haitians, Dominicans, Indians, Vietnamese, Iranians, Cubans, Chinese, and Laotians. These immigrants find American culture much different from their own. So they tend to group together in cities, forming their own societies and subcultures. For example, many Vietnamese have settled in California and many Arabs now live in Michigan.

Does America benefit as a pluralistic society—a society made of different groups? Or is it better off with a single cultural identity? Should we all eat the same kinds of foods, wear the same types of clothing, and speak the same language? These concerns are not new. In 1751, Benjamin Franklin worried about the influx of Germans in the Pennsylvania colony. He wrote: "This Pennsylvania will in a few years become a German colony; instead of their learning our language, we must learn theirs, or live as in a foreign country." Replace the word "German" with the name of any other large immigrant group today, and you have the arguments some people now offer for curbing immigration.

To varying degrees, your own horizons have been broadened by immigration in America. You may have enjoyed street fairs or food festivals where international dishes were served. You might have eaten Greek gyros, Italian pizza, Middle Eastern falafel, Mexican tacos, or Chinese noodles. Even the foods most thought of as "American"—frank-furters and hamburgers, came from Frankfurt and Hamburg, Germany, as their names indicate. Foreign culture continues to affect America. In 1993, ketchup was surpassed by salsa, a spicy Latin sauce, as the most widely sold condiment in the United States.

Is Patriotism Still Strong?   Immigrants may succeed in teaching Americans to value foreign culture. But what about the reverse? Do immigrants learn to

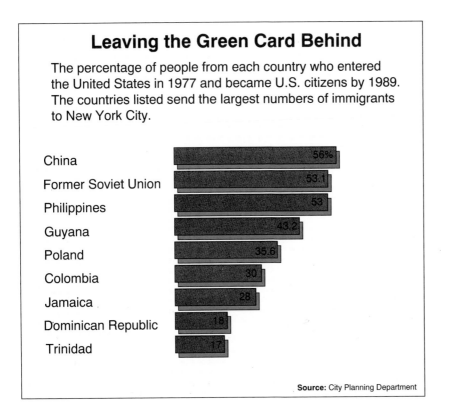

Leaving the Green Card Behind

The percentage of people from each country who entered the United States in 1977 and became U.S. citizens by 1989. The countries listed send the largest numbers of immigrants to New York City.

Country	Percentage
China	56%
Former Soviet Union	53.1
Philippines	53
Guyana	43.2
Poland	35.6
Colombia	30
Jamaica	28
Dominican Republic	18
Trinidad	17

Source: City Planning Department

appreciate American life as well? Do they demonstrate patriotism for their new home and government?

Some people say no. They point to statistics indicating that only about one third of all immigrants apply for U.S. citizenship. While immigrants reap the social and economic benefits of America, they argue, most do not participate in government. But pro-immigration groups disagree. They say that many immigrants cannot afford to become citizens, because they will then be barred from returning to their homeland. Others are afraid of taking the citizenship exam. But this does not always reflect their feelings of admiration and love for America.

Experts at the INS and other government agencies believe that more immigrants will seek U.S. citizenship in the future. Without the right to vote or serve on juries, they will never improve their situation, noncitizens say. Reflecting this changing attitude is Armando Espinosa, an Ecuadorean immigrant who never thought that he would apply for American citizenship. "I am Ecuadorean in my blood and my gut," he said. "I do not even like apple pie." Yet Armando Espinosa has now applied to be an American citizen. He explains, "If people like me retain our allegiances to home and refuse to participate in electoral politics here, the lot of our race will never improve."

Is Immigration Good for Europe?

The United States is not the only nation questioning the benefits of immigration. In the 1990s, many governments in Western Europe began passing new laws to stop the flow of newcomers to their countries. Their actions reversed a longtime European tradition of welcoming immigrants with open arms.

In 1993, the government of Germany revised its Constitution to prevent large numbers of political refugees from entering the country. In France, the interior minister announced a national goal of "zero immigration." And in Greece, the government rounded up and expelled 25,000 Albanians.

What has motivated these new policies of restriction? Partly it is to protect foreigners from increasing attacks on them by neo-Nazis, skinheads, and other radical groups. In Madrid, gangs have broken into buildings where Dominican squatters were living and shot them. In Rome, "Nazi-skins" have beaten up and burned Africans sleeping in the park.

Another reason for the restrictions is concern with rising unemployment. As in America, many in Europe believe that reducing immigration will help to improve the job market for native-born citizens.

But as in America, not everyone agrees. Some Western Europeans feel that the new policies betray a moral obligation that their countries have to those in need. Of course, would-be immigrants agree. In 1993, thousands of Liberians fled to Germany after three years of civil war in their own country. Worrying about being deported to Liberia, refugee Ali Ibrahim Jackson said in a *New York Times* interview, "I can't go back. I walk the street and I'm a dead man."

A neo-Nazi skinhead inside their headquarters in Rome, Italy.

5

Coping with Immigration Issues

As immigration to America continues, problems will arise—for government officials, local communities, and the new arrivals themselves. No one knows yet how each challenge will be handled. Americans have many questions to answer: How much money should be spent on social programs for immigrants? How should schools be made to accommodate foreign students? What kinds of hiring policies should employers follow?

The immigrants, on the other hand, ask another set of questions: How do we adapt to a new culture and language? How do we overcome the prejudices of our neighbors? How do we make a positive contribution to American

Hispanic schoolchildren salute the American flag. Foreign language programs for non-English-speaking children versus an English-only rule in school is a topic of concern among parents and educators.

society? By exploring some of these questions, you will be better able to form your own opinions about immigration.

Economic

Burden Should more money be spent for the housing, food, and medical needs of immigrants? That depends on whom you ask. Anti-immigration groups say no, claiming that the financial burden is already too great. Immigrants, they feel, create a tax deficit Americans cannot afford to bear. Donald Huddle, an immigration expert at Rice University, calculated that the 19 million immigrants who have entered the United States since 1970 used about $50 billion in government services in 1992. Yet they paid only about $20 billion in taxes the same year. That leaves a loss of $30 billion for American taxpayers to absorb. In 1993, California officials said it cost them $3 billion annually to provide welfare, medical care, and schooling—for illegals alone. "The state is broke," said one California assembly aide in a *Time* magazine interview. "We've had a multibillion-dollar deficit three years in a row, and yet we continue to pay medical benefits for these illegal immigrants. We take better care of them than of our own people."

Other groups disagree. They argue that immigrants, legal or not, deserve government benefits.

Legal aliens, they say, pay taxes and put more into the system than they take out. Even illegals, they add, contribute to the economy through their labor. Their work increases the supply of goods and services. And their spending increases a demand for other goods and services. In other words, immigrants create *more* jobs, not fewer. After these newcomers arrive, they require food, clothing, housing, and medical care. These basic needs result in jobs for those who provide them. Many people advocate spending on immigrants simply as a moral obligation. As one doctor explained, "We want them to clean our houses, rake our leaves, take care of our children, do the scut work of life. But if they get sick, we don't want to take care of them."

Language Barrier

Many people feel America's greatest immigration problem in the future will not be money, but language. The newest arrivals to the United States are from countries where almost no English is spoken. And many find English hard to learn. As a result, there are communication problems—in school, at work, and in the street. Some stories may seem humorous: One Russian library aide living in America panicked when three women came in and asked, "Can we cut through here?" She feared they wanted to cut up the books.

A daughter helps her father read and understand the information in an American newspaper. The language barrier is an increasing problem due to the large number of non-English-speaking people in the United States.

But the real language problems are no laughing matter. Some American schools are finding it difficult to provide teachers and textbooks for their students. In Los Angeles, Hispanics make up 65 percent of the city's public school population. In one school, the rate is 93 percent. Most of the children have difficulty with English. Yet less than one third of the teachers can speak Spanish. As a result, the Los Angeles school board agreed to hire 20 teachers from Mexico for the 1993–1994 school year. In Dade County, Florida, officials face similar problems. Some 75,000 non-English-speaking children fill the public schools there. It costs the county $80 million a year for special programs in foreign languages.

Some people feel the solution is to enforce an English-only rule in school. And they propose a similar measure for adults: Declare English the official language of the United States. That means that all business would have to be conducted in English alone. Others say such plans are impractical, if not illegal. If children don't know English, how will they understand it in school? And if America is a democracy, can people really be forced to conform to one language?

Still, some districts have been trying out this plan. In 1980, Dade County passed a law making English

A Lesson in Survival and Success

If anyone knows about the struggles of making it in America, it is Berenice Belizaire. In 1987, Berenice moved to New York City from Haiti. It was a very difficult adjustment. In Haiti, her family had owned a large house. Now they had to manage in a crowded apartment. At home, Berenice had been an excellent student. But in New York City, school was a nightmare. Speaking no English, Berenice was often the target of ridicule by her junior high classmates. Some cursed her and even threw food at her in the school cafeteria.

Berenice's mother told her daughter not to become discouraged. She reminded her of the importance of getting a good education, and urged her to "memorize everything." Over the next few years, Berenice did just that. In time, classmates discovered that Berenice always seemed to know the answers, and they even began asking her for help with their schoolwork. Her high school math teacher said, "She could think on her feet. She could explain difficult problems so the other kids could understand them."

By her senior year, Berenice ranked number one in her class, and graduated as valedictorian. Being very shy, she almost rejected the honor, and would not let her picture appear in the class yearbook. But she has since become more self-confident and assertive. After graduation, she entered Massachusetts Institute of Technology. Her goal? "I want to build a famous computer, like IBM. I want my name to be a part of it."

the sole language for official business. And in 1988, the states of Florida, Colorado, and Arizona declared English their official language. Yet many others reject the idea. In 1989, New Mexico voted against making English its official language. And in 1993, in Dade County, where 60 percent of the residents are Spanish-speaking, the old 1980 law was repealed.

A Chinese gang roams the streets in New York City's Chinatown. Anti-immigrationists believe that immigrants are responsible for much of U.S. crime.

Immigrants and Crime

In a 1993 *USA Today/CNN/Gallup* poll, 62 percent of those questioned said they believed immigrants contribute significantly to crime. Some statistics may even support their perceptions. In 1992, in Southern California, for example, at least 25 percent of the jail population was illegal aliens. In the first half of 1993, Chinese gangs were involved in six out of eight major heroin busts in the United States. Police say some alien groups are heavily involved in gun smuggling, prostitution, and gambling. Many fear that crime will become a serious by-product of immigration.

Some say that the American government is partly responsible for the crime brought by immigrants. They say that unguarded borders make entry for criminals too easy. Others feel that laws are too lenient. They point, for example, to the incident of the "Marielitos." In 1980, when many Cubans fled to Miami to seek political asylum, Cuban leader Fidel Castro took advantage of the situation. He expelled 125,000 Cubans from the city of Mariel, many of whom arrived on Florida's coast. Only after accepting them did U.S. officials discover that many were convicts from Cuban prisons. Although some were arrested and sent back to Cuba, many stayed in the United States and went on to commit more crimes.

Other groups contend that immigrants do not contribute significantly to crime. In fact, they claim that immigrants are more often the victims of crime than the perpetrators. Because they do not know the language or the "ways of the street," aliens have frequently fallen prey to attack. Some fear that anti-immigration sentiment could lead to increased violence against foreigners in America, as it has in Germany in the 1990s.

Fidel Castro.

The Debate Over Bilingual Education

For the past 25 years, Americans have argued this question: Should immigrants who speak little or no English be taught in their native languages in American schools? Educators are sharply divided on the issue.

In 1968, the U.S. Congress passed a law called the Bilingual Education Act. It set up special programs for students whose native language is not English. The goal was to help children ease their way into English by learning partly in their native language.

Many people immediately opposed the plan. Teachers unable to speak their students' native languages saw it as a threat to their jobs. Some parents felt it slowed down classroom learning for children already proficient in English. And others felt it hurt students' chances of getting a job in the "outside world" after finishing school. Many people lobbied to have bilingual education stopped. But in 1974, the U.S. Supreme Court ruled that children who do not know English are entitled to special treatment. The bilingual programs continued.

Twenty-five years later, the debate also continues. Those who oppose bilingual education say it has not been effective. In one example they cite, a large New York company gave an English-language test to 7,000 applicants. Only 4,000 passed, and not one applicant was from a bilingual school program. But others say that the programs are necessary so immigrant children do not become completely lost in the classroom. As one Asian student said, "It helped me survive in the new world."

What Will the Future Hold?

Amid the problems being faced, will American immigration continue to rise? During 1992, the United States accepted more immigrants than all other industrialized nations combined. That year, there were 100,000 requests for asylum alone. And there were 300,000 backlogged requests for asylum. By contrast, Canada had 37,000 requests for asylum in 1992. But its current acceptance rate of 51 percent is even higher than the U.S. rate of 36 percent. Thousands of refugees, especially from Somalia and Sri Lanka, now wait to be accepted by Canada. And more are

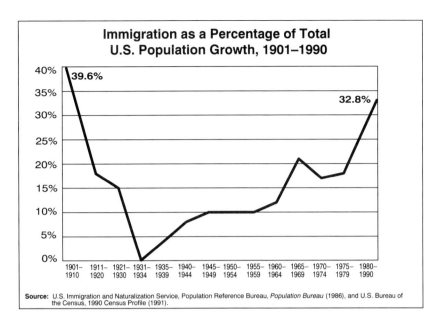

Immigration as a Percentage of Total U.S. Population Growth, 1901–1990

39.6%

32.8%

| 1901– | 1911– | 1921– | 1931– | 1935– | 1940– | 1945– | 1950– | 1955– | 1960– | 1965– | 1970– | 1975– | 1980– |
| 1910 | 1920 | 1930 | 1934 | 1939 | 1944 | 1949 | 1954 | 1959 | 1964 | 1969 | 1974 | 1979 | 1990 |

Source: U.S. Immigration and Naturalization Service, Population Reference Bureau, *Population Bureau* (1986), and U.S. Bureau of the Census, 1990 Census Profile (1991).

expected to line up after that. Unless new laws are adopted, immigration to both the United States and Canada seems likely to climb in the future.

How will all this change the face of America? In 1980, about 80 percent of the nation was white. But experts predict that by the year 2000, Americans of white European descent will be less than half of the population. By 2056, the "average" U.S. citizen will be from Africa, Asia, Central or South America, the Pacific Islands, or the Middle East.

A changing society brings changing attitudes with it. You are a part of that society. Should America maintain its tradition of sheltering "the tired, the poor, the huddled masses"? Or is it time to adopt a more restrictive immigration policy? Consider both sides of the issues carefully. Then make the fairest decision that you can.

Glossary

alien A foreigner, or a noncitizen resident in a country.

asylum Special status, or protection, given to aliens who can prove a threat of persecution if they were to return to their homeland.

deportation The legal expulsion of an illegal alien or criminal from a country.

green card (alien registration card) An identity card certifying the permanent resident status of an alien in the United States.

illegal alien An immigrant who has entered the country without registering with the proper authorities or who has falsified documents in order to enter.

immigration The act of entering a country to establish permanent residence there.

Immigration and Naturalization Service A division of the U.S. Department of Justice. It is the agency that enforces the immigration laws and policies set by Congress.

nativism An anti-immigration movement that took place in the middle 1800s. Nativists sought to restrict immigration to the United States and to limit participation of immigrants in the political affairs of the country.

naturalization The official process by which immigrants acquire citizenship in their new country.

pluralism The existence in a society of groups that differ in ethnic origin and cultural patterns.

quota The number or proportion of immigrants that is allowed to be admitted into a country.

refugee A person who flees his or her homeland to seek protection elsewhere, due to suffering such as war, religious or political persecution, disease, or famine.

visa An official permit issued by government authorities that allows legal entry into a country.

For Further Reading

Bode, Janet. *New Kids on the Block.* New York: Franklin Watts, 1989.

Bouvier, Leon. *Think About Immigration.* New York: Walker and Company, 1988.

Day, Carol Olsen and Day, Edmund. *The New Immigrants.* New York: Franklin Watts, 1985.

Dixon, Edward and Galan, Mark. *The Immigration and Naturalization Service.* New York: Chelsea House Publishers, 1990.

Stein, R. Conrad. *Ellis Island.* Chicago: Childrens Press, 1992.

Time (Special Issue). "The New Face of America," Fall 1993.

Source Notes

"America: Still a Melting Pot?" *Newsweek,* August 9, 1993, pp. 16-26.

Bouvier, Leon. *Think About Immigration.* New York: Walker and Company, 1988.

Dixon, Edward and Galan, Mark. *The Immigration and Naturalization Service.* New York: Chelsea House Publishers, 1990.

Dudley, William, ed. *Immigration: Opposing Viewpoints.* San Diego, CA: Greenhaven Press, 1990.

Puente, Maria. "Sentiment Sours as Rate of Arrival Rises." *USA Today,* July 14, 1993, p. 1.

"The Price of Open Arms." *Business Week,* June 21, 1993, pp. 32-35.

"Send Back Your Tired, Your Poor." *Time,* June 21, 1993, pp. 26-27.

Weiner, Tim. "Smuggled to New York; Fixing Immigration." *The New York Times,* June 8, 1993, p. B2.

Index

AIDS, 22
Alien registration card.
   See Green Card.
Amnesty, 36
Anti-immigration groups, 5, 20, 40, 52
Aristide, Reverend Jean-Bertrand, 22
Asylum, 36, 58
   definition of, 10
   political, 15, 29–30, 35, 57

Baird, Zoe, 33
Baline, Israel. *See* Irving Berlin.
Bangkok, Thailand, 8
Beijing, China, 15
Belizaire, Berenice, 55
Bell, Alexander Graham, 43
Berlin, Irving, 43
Bilingual Education Act, 58

Castro, Fidel, 57
Chinese Exclusion Act, 18
Clinton, Bill, 33, 36
Coast Guard, 8, 29

Einstein, Albert, 43
Ellis Island, 25
Emigration, 10, 15

Franklin, Benjamin, 46

Gentlemen's Agreement, 18
Golden Venture, The, 7, 9, 10, 11, 34–35

Green cards, 21, 23, 33, 47
Guantanamo Naval Base, 22

Helton, Arthur, 39
Huddle, Donald, 52

Illegal aliens, 11, 20, 27, 29–37, 40, 41,
   52–53
Immigrants
   Chinese, 7–9, 13, 15, 18, 29, 30, 35
   citizenship of, 10, 23–24, 48
   and crime, 56–57
   economic burden of, 52–53
   language barrier of, 53–56
   legal, 10, 21, 23, 27, 36, 53
   passports of, 10, 25, 29
   permanent residence of, 10, 21, 23, 24
   slavery and, 11, 32
   smuggling of, 7, 30, 32
   visas of, 10, 29, 37
Immigration
   definition of, 9–10
   forced, 10–11, 12
   illegal, 28–30, 35, 36
     dangers of, 30, 32
   laws, 15, 17, 18, 19–20, 24
   quotas, 18–19, 20
   racism and, 5, 19
   terrorism and, 39–40
   waves of, 12–14, 43
   zero, 49

Photo Credits

Cover: AP/Wide World Photos; p. 5: ©Blackbirch Press, Inc.; p. 6: ©Christensen/Gamma-Liaison; p. 8: ©Filipacchi/Gamma-Liaison; p. 11: Culver Pictures, Inc.; p. 12: AP/Wide World Photos; p. 15: Associated Press; p. 16: ©Andrew Holbrooke/Gamma-Liaison; p. 19: Culver Pictures, Inc.; p. 20: ©1988 Zigy Kaluzny/Gamma-Liaison; p. 21: ©Paul Howell/Gamma-Liaison; p. 22: ©Fred Francis/Gamma-Liaison; p. 23: Wide World Photos; p. 25: Wide World Photos; p. 26: Associated Press; p. 28: ©P. Chartrand/Gamma-Liaison; p. 31: AP/Wide World Photos; p. 33: AP/Wide World Photos; p. 35: Gamma-Liaison; p. 36: AP/Wide World Photos; p. 37: AP/Wide World Photos; p. 38: AP/Wide World Photos; p. 41: AP/Wide World Photos; p. 42: ©Blackbirch Press, Inc.; p. 43: AP Newsfeatures; p. 45: ©Blackbirch Press, Inc.; p. 49: Massimo Sestini/Gamma-Liaison; p. 50: ©Spencer Grant/Liaison International; p. 54: ©Stuart Rabinowitz; p. 56: Wide World Photos; p. 57: ©Pablo Azarra/Gamma-Liaison.
Graphs by Lisa Willis.